FUTURISTICS

FUTURISTICS

A
FIRST
BOOK

LILLIAN BIERMANN WEHMEYER

FRANKLIN WATTS 1986
NEW YORK LONDON TORONTO SYDNEY

Charts and graphs by Vantage Art, Inc.

Photographs courtesy of:
The Bettmann Archive: pp. 4, 7, 14, 16;
NASA: pp. 28, 29.

Library of Congress Cataloging in Publication Data

Wehmeyer, Lillian Biermann, 1933—
  Futuristics.

  (A First book)
  Bibliography: p.
  Includes index.
  Summary: Discusses futurists, from psychics to
economists and philosophers, and the ways they study
the past and present in order to forecast the future.
I. Title.
    1. Forecasting—Juvenile literature.   [1. Forecasting]
  CB158.W44 1986   303.4'9   85-26315
  ISBN 0-531-10116-9

CONTENTS

ACKNOWLEDGMENT

To Mrs. Gwen Batey and
her advanced English class
at Turnbull Middle School,
San Mateo, California, for
their critique of an early
draft of this manuscript.

CHAPTER 1
FROM
FORTUNE-TELLERS
TO FUTURISTS

What do you think when someone mentions the future? Perhaps you imagine events of tomorrow, next month, next year, or a thousand years from now. Tomorrow you may appear on stage in a school play, win a championship football game, celebrate your birthday, or write an important report. A century from now people may live in a space colony on the moon, or inside enormous satellites orbiting the earth. Cancer may have disappeared, as smallpox has already. Typhoons may be shrunk to small rain-storms through the use of new technology to control weather. Citizens may press a few keys on a computer every week or so to tell the government their opinions on important issues. Many exciting possibilities come to mind, perhaps along with mistakes and tragedies.

This is a book about ways people look at the future. FUTURISTS are people who study information about the past and present in order to forecast some of the many futures that might happen. Then they recommend ways for governments, business corporations, or other groups to work toward the future possibilities that seem best. However, let us begin by talking about people who tried to see into the future before futuristics was ever thought of—people such as fortune-tellers, prophets, and the "imagineers" who create science fiction stories and films.

PREDICTING THE FUTURE

Before you read further, stop for a moment and list all the ways you know that are now used, or have been used in the past, to predict the future. How many methods do you remember?

Here is my list. Did you think of the same ones?

- looking into a crystal ball
- palm reading, or telling someone's fortune from the lines in the palm of the hand
- reading tea leaves
- consulting with an astrologer or a PSYCHIC
- asking an ORACLE
- PHRENOLOGY, or studying the shape of the head
- fortune-telling with a deck of cards
- numerology, or converting names and dates to numbers, each number having a certain meaning.

Futurists are not likely to think of any of the methods on my list as a reliable means of predicting the future. In fact, they prefer to speak of "forecasting possible futures" rather than "predicting THE future." They regard the methods listed above, and others described in this chapter, as "unscientific." What does it mean to say that something is not scientific?

Let us define "scientific" as describing <u>the method of research in which a hypothesis, formed after systematic, objective collection of information, is investigated by experiment or observation.</u>

The most important words in this definition are:

SYSTEMATIC,
OBJECTIVE,
INVESTIGATE,
EXPERIMENT OR OBSERVATION.

A method that is NOT scientific is NOT systematic, NOT objective, and NOT investigated by experiment or observation. Of course, even the "purest" of sciences is not completely systematic, objective, or always able to be investigated—as we shall discuss in the next chapter. To begin with, however, let us consider some older methods of predicting the future and then check back to see how well they fit the definition of "scientific."

First, suppose that you are a commander, leading an army to battle in ancient Greece. You want to know whether you will win or lose if you attack the enemy tomorrow. What might you do? If the battle is very important, and if you have time for a short trip, you may visit an oracle.

ORACLES AND DIVINERS

The word ORACLE means both a PLACE where a god or goddess was thought to reveal the future and the PERSON who announced such predictions. Ancient Egyptians and Hebrews consulted oracles, but the most famous oracle was located in Greece on the side of Mount Parnassus at a place called DELPHI. This oracle, which was very well known about twenty-five hundred years ago, has given futurists a name for one of their modern techniques, as we shall see in chapter 3. The temple at Delphi was dedicated to Apollo, the Greek god of music and prophecy. According to tradition, Apollo's priestess prophesied while sitting in an underground chamber where she inhaled and was intoxicated by vapors rising naturally from the earth. However, archaeologists have thus far been unable to find evidence of such vapors at the temple's location. The priestess, or Pythia, chewed laurel leaves and inhaled incense to help herself go into a trance. Her predictions sometimes came out as a meaningless string of words, so a priest stood by to explain her prophecy.

Unfortunately, the advice of an oracle was not always helpful, even after a priest interpreted it, because a prophecy could have more than one meaning. For example, this story is told about Croesus, who was king of a country called Lydia. (Have you ever heard anyone say that a very wealthy person is "as rich as Croesus"? It is to this king they are referring.)

Croesus expanded his kingdom by conquering lands surrounding Lydia. Eventually he was ready to go to war with Cyrus,

Pythia, the famous Grecian oracle,
is consulted by the priests.

King of Persia. Croesus consulted the oracle at Delphi and received this answer: "When you cross the river Halys, you will destroy a great empire." Encouraged by this prophecy, Croesus led his army across the Halys to do battle with the Persian soldiers. Unfortunately, Croesus had not considered that the great empire which he would destroy might be his own Kingdom of Lydia—but that is exactly what happened. His soldiers were defeated, and Croesus himself was captured by the Persian king. Clearly, one had to be careful in using the advice of an oracle!

Then, was an oracle scientific? We said that the information collected by a scientific method is SYSTEMATIC and OBJECTIVE. But systematic and objective information should try for one clear meaning. An oracle was expected to predict THE future—just one future. But the prediction could have exactly opposite meanings, as happened with Croesus. Therefore, it was not scientific. Such advice was not very useful, either, so eventually people stopped going to oracles.

Gods and goddesses were believed to communicate through other means in addition to oracles. A priest might use objects like dice or cards to assist in telling the future. Anyone who used methods like these was called a DIVINER, a person who could prophesy the future.

Some priests and priestesses at Delphi used methods of DIVINATION, especially for those people who were not important enough to have their questions answered by the Pythia herself. To give advice to these less important visitors, Delphic priests used a system of drawing lots. For instance, if a visitor asked a question that could be answered simply yes or no, a priest would shake a container and pull out a single bean. A white bean meant yes; a black bean meant no.

Some diviners used a chicken to look into the future. Sand was marked off into sections—one space for each letter of the alphabet. Grain was strewn on the sand and a hungry hen or cock turned loose. As the chicken ate each grain, someone wrote down the letter in that section of sand. As you can imagine, these letters usually did not form words, so a priest or other diviner would examine the letters, decide what words were meant, and announce the message.

Besides beans and chickens, other objects which have been used by diviners include dice, tea leaves, the palm of the hand, dominoes, and cards (either regular playing cards or special fortune-telling cards called TAROT CARDS).

As time passed, people no longer believed in the old gods and goddesses, so they explained the methods of diviners in terms of the interconnectedness of all things. In other words, those who use such items to foretell the future (again, just one future) believe that all things are connected to one another so that small things reflect the larger world. Palm reading is based on this belief.

Palm reading, also called CHIROMANCY, has been used for about four thousand years. Palm readers believe that the small lines in the palm of a person's hand form a miniature picture or map of the life of that person. Detailed reference books explain features of the palm such as the "lifeline" and the "Mount of Jupiter." Such books contain statements about the relationship of the lines and shape of the palm to the future life of that person. These statements might be regarded as HYPOTHESES. But where is the systematic and objective information? Who has investigated to see how dependable these relationships really are? Since palm readers and other diviners attempt to predict just one future, and since they predict from relationships that have not been demonstrated, most scientists regard such methods as unscientific.

Suppose again that you are a commander in ancient Greece and you do not have time to consult an oracle, nor do you want to try a diviner. What else might you do? Perhaps you would want to call in your astrologer.

ASTROLOGERS

Like palm reading, astrology is about four thousand years old. It was used in ancient Mesopotamia, where Chaldean priests studied the stars and planets with great care. Had a commander

Two Roman diviners who used caged birds to predict the future. If the birds when they were released flew to the left, good fortune followed; if to the right, evil times ahead were indicated.

turned to his astrologer for advice, the astrologer would already have plotted the positions of the heavenly bodies at the moment the commander was born. Now he would examine the positions of those same heavenly bodies for the following day and cast a horoscope.

In modern times, the positions of stars and planets, once obtained from reference books and charts, are now programmed into computers so that one need only input a date, time, and place to find out how the bodies were or will be positioned.

Having studied the positions of the heavenly bodies, an astrologer examines their meaning. Each star or planet is believed to influence people in specific ways. Not only that, but the heavenly bodies also interact with one another. Therefore, the astrologer must consider how much the commander's sun sign—Aquarius, Scorpio, or another of the twelve signs of the zodiac—is being influenced by the positions of the moon and planets.

An astrologer studies a long time to understand the charts, mathematical formulas, and other materials which describe effects of heavenly bodies on people's lives. Even the word "astrology" ends like "biology" and other names of sciences. Astrology has helped science in several ways. First, astrologers studied the positions of the stars and planets very carefully; these observations became the basis for the science of astronomy. Second, astrologers helped develop the mathematical systems upon which science depends. Finally, astrology introduced the very scientific notion that some things in the natural world cause other things to happen. Nevertheless, most scientists think astrology is not a science. They reject it because astrologers predict THE future—just one future—and because no one has systematically and objectively gathered information about the relationship between heavenly bodies and people's lives.

Do you recall why diviners and astrologers believe their methods work? Remember, diviners believe that all things are connected so that small things provide a picture of the larger world. Astrologers say that the heavenly bodies influence our lives. Most scientists believe these methods are unscientific, but astrologers and diviners themselves believe their explanations are scientific and enable them to predict the future.

PSYCHICS

Other individuals also claim to see into the future. They say they are PSYCHICS who have the power of PRECOGNITION, which means the ability to see or hear future events before they occur. Precognition is just one form of extrasensory perception, or ESP for short.

Some psychics have volunteered to work with scientists who study precognition and other forms of ESP. These scientists have devised experiments to test the accuracy of ESP and to find out how it works. So far it has proved very difficult to establish scientific evidence regarding ESP.

Sometimes dishonest people claim to be psychics. For example, early in 1981 President Ronald Reagan was shot and wounded. The next day national television broadcasts showed a videotape, supposedly made before the attack on the president, in which a psychic predicted that event. It was soon learned, however, that the so-called prediction had been taped AFTER, rather than before, the shooting. Despite such difficulties, scientists continue to study ESP.

Sometimes people get together just for fun to see whether they have psychic powers. This writer had such an experience at the age of about thirteen years old. We were visiting relatives. Several adults and children sat around a card table to see if we could persuade a spirit to speak to us. We all pressed our fingertips on the tabletop and chanted "Up table, up table" over and over until finally—to my surprise—the legs on one side of the table did lift up off the floor.

"Spirit, are you there? Tap once for yes and twice for no," someone whispered. The leg tapped once. We were so startled, and perhaps just a bit frightened, that we moved our hands and "lost contact." The table was again firmly standing on all four legs, and we had no opportunity to ask more questions.

What really happened? Some people might say . . .

- we really talked to the spirit of a dead person, or
- someone was playing a trick on us, or
- we all gradually pressed in the same direction, without realizing it, until we lifted the table a little bit.

How would you explain it? Scientists have not yet figured out what ESP is—or even whether it is real. Until they do, most scientists will avoid ESP as a way to find out about the future.

Some people who look into the future, on the other hand, do not even want to be thought of as scientific. They are the religious prophets.

PROPHETS

The gods that were associated with Greek oracles no longer have followers today. But other religions have had PROPHETS of their own, especially Judaism, Christianity, and Islam. Prophets in these religions have usually received their messages in visions which they later described.

Consider the Jewish prophet Isaiah, for example. About twenty-seven hundred years ago he wrote that one day when he went to the temple, he "saw the Lord sitting upon a throne, high and lifted up" and surrounded by six-winged angels. When an angel called out, Isaiah tells us, "the foundations of the thresholds shook at the voice of him who called, and the house was filled with smoke." Then an angel took a burning coal from the altar in the temple and flew to Isaiah, touching his mouth with the coal. At that moment Isaiah knew that he had been chosen to speak as a prophet for the God of the Hebrew people.

Prophets of these major religions did not always announce future events. Often, they advised the people what to do right at that time. Sometimes they warned that if their followers did not obey God's message, the consequences would be awful; but if they obeyed, the awful future would change for the better.

Some religious prophecies speak of the end of this world and a better world to come. Ancient Germanic peoples, for example, believed in Ragnarök, the defeat of the gods. According to one story, this defeat would be followed by a new earth where Balder, son of the supreme god Odin, would rule while good men would live forever in a hall of gold.

Another prophecy of the end of the world is found in the Book of Revelation, the last book in the Christian Bible. This book, written about fifty or sixty years after Jesus' death, describes wars and suffering, after which Jesus is to return to earth to judge all men, taking those who accept him as their savior to a new heaven and a new earth, where they will live forever.

Religious groups do not claim their prophets are scientific. Quite the opposite—a prophet is regarded as a very unusual person who is certainly not to be INVESTIGATED or EXPERIMENTED with. Believers in Judaism, Christianity, and Islam believe their prophets bring them truths far more important than the findings of science—truths that help them deal with whatever the future may bring.

THE IDEA OF PROGRESS

PHILOSOPHERS are people who think a good deal about why things are and how they should be. Some philosophers thought about the religious idea that God or gods will bring about a grand finale to history, then changed that idea into a belief that history has its own laws of development. About 1807 the German philosopher Georg Friedrich Hegel wrote about a Spirit which realizes itself in history—a Spirit that is more like a force, say electric energy, than a god. This Spirit, according to Hegel, drives history from one stage to the next. Often the Spirit works through a particular leader like Julius Caesar, who conquered much of the ancient Roman Empire, or Napoleon Bonaparte, who for a short time during the nineteenth century brought most of continental Europe under the rule of France.

Hegel's ideas were used by the philosopher Karl Marx, who thought that the laws of history would lead to the downfall of industrial capitalism and the establishment of a system owned by the workers themselves. This system, Marx believed, would be a perfect, communist society. Marx's ideas were used in the

Russian revolution of 1917. Marx's perfect society has not emerged in Russia, but Russians turned their attention to the future with a series of five-year plans to increase production on farms and in factories. Noncommunist countries, industrial corporations, and even schools have also developed multi-year plans.

Meanwhile, scientists were developing new theories which would help change how people think about the future and inspire the writers and artists sometimes called IMAGINEERS. First, geologists studied rocks and fossils and decided that the earth was not merely six thousand years old, as people had previously thought. Instead, they believed the earth had formed over four or five billion years by erosion, earthquakes, and volcanoes. Then, about 1850, Charles Darwin and other biologists developed a theory to explain how animals and plants might have evolved, that is, changed over three billion years from simple cells to all the varieties of life on earth today.

The idea of evolution of the earth and living things had an important effect on people's ideas of the future. For if the world had evolved in the past, people thought, it would certainly continue to do so in the future. And since the earth seemed more comfortable than when it had been hot and covered by water— and since humankind seemed more marvelous than bacteria or amoebae—it was easy to suppose that everything would get better and better. Religion, philosophy, and science all agreed that the world was going somewhere. People began to believe in progress. Perhaps, eventually, our world would really be perfect.

IMAGINEERS

Just think of writing stories, articles, or books during the time when these ideas were being discussed. No wonder that people began to imagine a perfect world and to write books about it! The most famous such book, UTOPIA, by Thomas More, had already been published in England in 1516, over three-hundred years before Hegel wrote about the Spirit of history. Thomas

More gave the name Utopia to the perfect country he described, and all such stories have been called UTOPIAS ever since.

Numerous utopian stories appeared in the 1800s when writers were inspired by the idea of progress. One of the best known of these was LOOKING BACKWARD: 2000 TO 1887, by Edward Bellamy. Newspaper reporters and artists described marvelous inventions of the future. Science fiction was established at the same time. The word IMAGINEERS has been coined to identify these people who used their imaginations to write descriptions and stories of the future.

One of the first important writers of science fiction was Jules Verne. This French novelist followed several utopian stories of his own with a successful series of adventure stories which mentioned fossils, electricity, a submarine, and a trip to the moon. His submarine story, TWENTY THOUSAND LEAGUES UNDER THE SEA, published in 1870, is the most popular.

Meanwhile, however, the idea of progress began to run into trouble almost as soon as it was created. Imagineers began to think of problems as well as progress.

Perhaps Earth would be conquered by evil aliens from another planet, as H. G. Wells imagined in his novel WAR OF THE WORLDS, published in 1898. Perhaps human beings will exist only to repair computer-mobiles, as described in a story entitled THE ENDLESS PAVEMENT. Such a pessimistic story is called a DYSTOPIA because it is the opposite of a utopia.

Or perhaps we will be forced to return to a simpler way of life, raising our own food and living without machines. Ruth Hooker tells such a story in her book KENNAQUHAIR, about survivors of nuclear war. A story of this type is called a PASTORAL UTOPIA. "Utopia" shows that the author prefers this simpler life. "Pastoral," which originally referred to shepherds, reminds us of people who live peacefully in the countryside.

Imagineers created thousands of ideas about the future. Some were just for fun. In 1912 Edgar Rice Burroughs, author of the Tarzan books, began a series describing the adventures of John Carter on Mars. Then came the first science fiction magazine, AMAZING STORIES, and the first science fiction comic

strip showing the adventures of Buck Rogers, set in the twenty-fifth century. The first comic book for science fiction was SUPERMAN, begun in 1938.

In that same year H. G. Wells's novel WAR OF THE WORLDS was dramatized on the radio in the form of "news flashes" about an invasion from Mars. Many listeners were terrified because they thought the invasion was really happening. Soon, however, people became used to science fiction on the radio, then in movies and finally on television.

Perhaps the most famous TV science fiction series is STAR TREK. The seventy-nine STAR TREK shows have continued as re-runs for twenty years. Fans of the series, called "Trekkies," make it their hobby, collect items related to the program, and meet together at conventions. New STAR TREK books and movies keep the fans interested.

"Special effects" using miniatures, computer techniques, and other tricks with cameras and film have created truly convincing science fiction worlds. The film STAR WARS used over 350 special effects. They were certainly successful, since people paid over $2.5 million to see the film in just the first week it was shown.

Imagineers and science have some connections. People who write science fiction books and produce science fiction films often use ideas borrowed from science. On the other hand, some scientists, including Carl Sagan, who produced the television

A woodcut from Jules Verne's 1870 novel TWENTY THOUSAND LEAGUES UNDER THE SEA, depicting the engine room of the submarine NAUTILUS, where the engine is electrically operated and the current is derived from a chemical reaction using sea water. The speed attempted with this fantastic vessel was 40 miles (64 km) per hour.

series and the book Cosmos, credit the reading of science fiction as an influence in their choice of careers. But imagineers usually are not scientists. The important thing to them is the story, and most writers of fiction will make up explanations, if necessary, to keep a story going.

In this chapter we have talked about many of the ways people have tried to look into the future. Many of these old ways still survive. But the idea of evolution and the many pictures of the future created by imagineers set the stage for a new approach. The time came for a more scientific way of studying the future than through the use of oracles, astrologers, or ESP.

In this illustration from H. G. Wells's novel War of the Worlds, a Martian war machine appears over London, poised for conquest.

[17]

CHAPTER 2
FUTURISTS

Forty years ago the word "futuristics" was not used (at least, not in the sense it is used today). But many people were becoming aware of an accelerated rate of change—in other words, the world was changing faster and faster. Of course, there have been other periods of change in history. Life was certainly changed for many people when the Black Death plague killed one out of every three people in Europe between 1346 and 1350. Wars, changes of government, and new religious ideas are among other events that rapidly changed people's lives. However, in earlier times such events happened only now and then. Therefore, children could usually expect to live in a world much like their parents'.

In the last two hundred years, on the other hand, certain changes have occurred more and more rapidly, especially changes due to technology. Inventions have followed one another so quickly that we have trouble keeping up with them. You might ask some older relatives or friends what has changed since they were children or since they held their first job.

Children who rode a horse to school grew up to drive an automobile, then fly in an airplane, and eventually see a man walk on the moon. Children who knew about the telegraph grew up listening to the radio and finally watched television. Some jobs became obsolete—no more iceman, no more elevator operator.

Meanwhile, new jobs were created: air traffic controller, computer engineer. A cartoon shows a little boy complaining about the effort he wasted learning to tie his shoes, only to find that he no longer needs to tie them because Velcro has been invented. Today even a seven-year-old finds himself with obsolete knowledge!

Figuring out the future ahead of time is even more important in a changing world. Beginning about the year 1900 writers produced books and magazine articles predicting the future of transportation, medicine, and other areas affected by technology. Some of their wrong guesses seem humorous today—trains powered by radio waves, and cars that park sideways. Still, change was all around, and we found we had to make decisions in that changing world.

DECIDING ABOUT
THE FUTURE

Have you thought of the life you want for yourself in the future? What decisions will you make? You may choose a school, a job to prepare for, someone to marry, and where to live. These are decisions about your personal future. Futuristics extends personal decision making to groups—a business corporation or a government agency, for example. Groups and individuals need not wait for the future to happen by accident. Instead, they can study possible futures, choose the best one, and then deliberately try to make it happen.

Such a group was set up by President Herbert Hoover in 1929. The National Resources Committee was not asked to study natural resources, but people resources. They were to analyze social changes in order to help the president propose laws for a better future.

Unfortunately, this optimistic beginning was followed quickly by the Great Depression—a time when stock market prices fell, banks closed, and one out of four Americans did not have a job. Unemployment insurance did not yet exist, so many people who had lost their jobs could not pay their rent or even buy groceries. How could such a disaster happen, people asked.

It turned out that at least some causes of the Great Depression could have been avoided. For example, the "crash" of the stock market, when prices of stocks fell so low that many wealthy individuals became poor in a single day, was due mostly to buying of stocks "on margin," that is, with money borrowed without proper backing. Once this was known, the government passed laws to limit purchases of stock with borrowed money. Have you ever said to yourself "If only I had realized. . . ." or "If only I had done. . . ."? After the Great Depression people thought, "If only we had passed these laws earlier." We were learning the hard way to look ahead to the future.

CHANGING THE FUTURE WITH R&D

The Second World War (1939–45) taught us another lesson about the future. Because of changing technology, leaders of all nations saw the importance of being first to produce more powerful weapons. In particular, Albert Einstein's theory of relativity suggested that nuclear fission—splitting the atom—could cause an enormous explosion. The race was on to develop an atomic bomb. The U.S. War Department set up the Manhattan Project for that purpose. The best experts worked together with the people and laboratories they needed and produced a bomb six hundred times more powerful than the "blockbuster" bomb, so named because it could flatten ten buildings in a city block. The Manhattan Project showed everyone that people can make things happen through research and development, which was soon nicknamed "R&D." Later, in 1961, President John Kennedy directed the National Aeronautics and Space Administration (NASA) to place a man on the moon and bring him back safely before 1970. The task was accomplished in July 1969.

Businesses also set up R&D departments to develop new products. They hired engineers and other specialists and told them what was needed—a better copying machine, or an automobile that would travel more miles per gallon of gas, for example. After trying several ideas, R&D people usually came up with a design that worked. R&D was changing the future. R&D was the beginning of futuristics.

Do you recall the steps in human thinking that have brought us to the beginning of futuristics? Here is a summary of the ideas we have talked about in this book.

1. We can try to predict the future with divination, astrology, and ESP.
2. At some time in the future the world will reach a final and perfect goal.
3. The future evolves gradually out of the past and present.
4. The world is gradually getting better and better—people called that "progress."
5. We can imagine many possible futures, not just one—and some of them are not better worlds, after all.
6. The world is changing more and more quickly, especially in technology.
7. If we plan for the future, we may avoid making mistakes.
8. We can study possible futures and choose the one we want.
9. After we decide on a future we want, we can make choices intended to help it happen—and happen sooner.
10. Those who study possible futures and how one possibility might be helped and another avoided are called "futurists."

THINK TANKS

When experts get together to study the future, they spend much of their time just thinking. So futurist organizations like R&D departments were nicknamed THINK TANKS. The RAND Corporation, one of the first and best-known think tanks, took its name from R&D: Research And Development = Rand. The Rand Corporation began as the R&D department of Douglas Aircraft Company. Soon after World War II, however, Rand began to study technological inventions in all areas. Rand developed the Delphi technique and the scenario, both of which are discussed in the next chapter of this book.

Futurists in think tanks study information about the past and present in order to think about the future. Soon, think tanks were publishing reports not just on technology, but also about changes in natural resources, government, foreign affairs, jobs, and even family life.

The more they studied the future, the more futurists found that thinking ahead about just one topic is not enough because things are interconnected. Futurists do not mean that small things reflect the larger world, as diviners thought, but that one change causes other changes. For example, the development of television reduced attendance at movies and other entertainment, the amount people read, and the extent of conversation within families, while at the same time it created new jobs for actors, advertising people, camera operators, and television sales people. No wonder that when Willis Harman, a futurist long associated with Stanford University in California, listed major events that could happen by the year 2000, he found twenty thousand combinations of these events. Twenty thousand is a large number of possible futures! As more and more topics were studied in think tanks, futuristics involved more and more people.

In 1966 the World Future Society was founded in Washington, D.C. The society publishes THE FUTURIST and other magazines. Within less than twenty years the society had thirty thousand members and listed local chapters in forty-nine states and twenty-three nations.

Two years later the Club of Rome was formed, bringing together individual scientists, businessmen, and politicians from around the world. Membership is limited to one hundred of the top people in these fields. The group's first report, entitled THE LIMITS TO GROWTH, was published in 1972. The report warned that if every business and every country keeps on trying to become larger and richer, catastrophe will result. THE LIMITS TO GROWTH pointed out that there is a limit to the amount of food to be harvested, a limit to supplies of oil, iron, and other resources, and a limit to the number of people who can live on earth. This rather pessimistic report became the basis for numerous books and articles, some agreeing and some disagreeing. The Club of Rome continued to sponsor reports, including GOALS FOR MANKIND, a more optimistic discussion of hopes for the future held by peoples around the world.

Reports like LIMITS TO GROWTH and GOALS FOR MANKIND quickly divided futurists into two groups whom we might call the optimists and the pessimists. But how can futurists contradict each other if futuristics is a science? Should not each study lead to similar results?

IS FUTURISTICS
A SCIENCE?

In chapter 1 we defined "scientific" as describing the method of research in which a hypothesis, formed after systematic, objective collection of data, is investigated by experiment or observation. In science, the same experiment is expected to turn out the same way no matter how many times it is repeated. If it does not, the scientist finds what elements in the experiment changed, or develops a new hypothesis. But sometimes many years pass during which a theory is believed true, until one day a scientist conducts an experiment or observation which forces a change in the theory. Heated arguments often go on in the meantime. Two such examples are the argument over whether the sun moves around the earth (of course, it does not) and whether light is made up of waves or of very small particles (it is both).

Sometimes a hypothesis is developed which cannot be proved or disproved for many years because no one can design an experiment to test it, or because the necessary technology is not yet available. For example, in 1915 astronomer Karl Schwarzschild used knowledge of stars and gravity to hypothesize "black holes." Then astronomers began searching for black holes in the heavens. As I write this, they have located several possible black holes, but no instruments are powerful enough for us to be certain. Perhaps by the time you read this page, black holes will have been proved real.

Sometimes a hypothesis cannot be proved or disproved for a long time because the object under study is so complex. For instance, figuring out what part of the human brain does what job is complicated by the fact that the brain contains some ten billion nerve cells, or neurons, and that neurons in various parts of the brain must work together even for one simple activity such as watching someone run.

Futurists also develop hypotheses which cannot be proved yet. They look for patterns in what has happened in the past in order to forecast possible futures. But because futuristics is a new science, the necessary information often has not been systematically collected for a long enough period of time so that patterns show up clearly. Besides, futuristics is very complex. In fact, if you take everything we know about the physical sciences and everything we know about biology, you must still add all the ways that individuals, groups, and nations act and interact in order to put together all the factors that affect futuristics. Remember those twenty thousand possible futures developed by Willis Harman!

And then, how does a futurist conduct an investigation? A physicist experiments with atomic particles in a laboratory. A biologist might study bacteria or mice. But just as an astronomer cannot move stars around because they are too far away, so a futurist cannot move people around because they will not stand for it. Astronomers solve some of their research problems with models—either real three-dimensional models or computer representations. With these models, astronomers "try out" movements of the stars and planets. If a model looks like what they see in telescopes, it becomes a sort of hypothesis. Next, astronomers use that model to predict other things in the heavens. These predictions are their experiments. If the predictions prove correct, the hypothesis is confirmed. This very procedure has led to a hypothesis that another planet lies out beyond Pluto, a planet which has been called "X." Have astronomers found Planet X yet?

You could do something similar with, say, a model railroad system. Suppose you want to figure out how to carry the largest possible number of passengers, or how to get the best schedule at each stop on the line. You could try different numbers and sizes of trains, faster and slower speeds, and so on. You could put this same information into a computer and program the computer to show the same arrangements you would try with a model railroad. Either way, you try your plans without touching a real railroad. If you make a mistake, model trains crash, not the real ones.

Futurists work with computer models much as astronomers do. But because futuristics is a young science, less than fifty years old, futurists' models are still incomplete. As time passes, futurists, like other scientists before them, will improve systems for collecting information, develop more objective methods, and continue to investigate their ideas by experiments with models and by careful observation of the world around them.

FUTURISTS DISAGREE

While futurists work on better information and methods, they will continue to disagree, just as scientists have disagreed about whether the earth moves around the sun and whether light is waves or particles. What are some of the disagreements among futurists?

One difference is that between optimists and pessimists. Do you usually look on the bright side, like an optimist, or are you more inclined to worry, like a pessimist? We have already mentioned the rather pessimistic views of Dennis Meadows, author of the Club of Rome report on limits to growth. Meadows sees little hope of avoiding a future of too many people, too much pollution, and not enough resources. Like religious prophets of olden times, pessimists warn us to change our ways to avoid catastrophe.

An optimist among futurists has been Herman Kahn. In THE NEXT 200 YEARS Kahn and his staff at the Hudson Institute (another think tank) argue that population growth will slow down as more nations become richer and that environmental problems will arise slowly enough for us to do something about them. They list possibilities for finding new mineral deposits, creating artificial materials, and other steps to keep us going until we are able to obtain needed materials from the moon or asteroids. But optimists also know we must work on these problems meanwhile.

Just as optimists disagree with pessimists, so earth-centered futurists also disagree with space-oriented futurists. Paul Ehrlich is an earth-centered futurist. He has written several scenarios to dramatize the results of pollution of the environment. Earth-centered futurists think of earth as a spaceship. They remind us that we have only one earth and we need to take care of it.

Space-oriented futurists focus on movement into outer space where, they believe, we will find both natural resources and living space. Gerard K. O'Neill of Princeton University, author of THE HIGH FRONTIER, is space-oriented. O'Neill predicts that within a hundred years more Americans will live in space colonies than on earth. These space colonies will be hollow metal balls, made of materials from the moon or asteroids. We might call these space colonies "outside-in" planets. Giant mirrors will reflect sunlight into the colony. A sphere will rotate slowly to create centrifugal force to "push" everything against the surface of the ball. Centrifugal force inside the ball will feel much like gravity, which holds us to the surface of the earth. At the "poles" of this outside-in planet, however, people will be able to float about and to play three-dimensional sports such as those described in some science fiction books. People in colonies will be busy manufacturing items from raw materials on the moon, asteroids, and other planets. Space colonists will also raise crops, make goods, and perform services for one another.

Right: An artist's conception
of a space colony in the shape
of a giant wheel. The central
hub contains the docking station
and communication antenna; six
spokes connect the hub with the
ring-shaped outer wheel and
provide entry and exit to living
and agricultural areas. Below:
The construction of an agricultural area. These farming
sections are interspersed with
more populated areas. The
louvers, shown being installed,
would absorb cosmic radiation,
while allowing sunlight to
be reflected inside.

Later colonies might be cylinder-shaped structures, about 10 miles (16 km) long and 4 miles (6 km) in diameter, housing several million people. Some futurists estimate that such colonies will be in place within the next fifty years.

Finally, just as pessimists disagree with optimists, and earth-centered futurists disagree with space-centered futurists, so EVOLUTIONISTS disagree with TRANSFORMATIONISTS. Daniel Bell, chairman of the Commission on the Year 2000, sponsored by the American Academy of Arts and Sciences in Boston, and editor for the book TOWARD THE YEAR 2000, is an evolutionist. He believes the future will develop gradually from the present, as the present has from the past. He points out how America's agricultural society of 1790 changed to an industrial society in the 1900s. Bell thought we would soon live in a post industrial society (POST means "after"). Here is a chart to show how his forecast is coming true:

| | PERCENT OF U.S. WORKERS | | |
YEAR	in agri-culture	in manu-facturing	in trade and services
1820	73	12	15
1980	3	29	68

How did most Americans make a living in 1820? in 1980? Today so many people work in communications, and other occupations that handle information that some futurists prefer the phrase "information society" to "post industrial society." Futuristics fits right into an information society, since futurists use information about past and present to forecast possible futures. Evolutionists see society changing little by little.

Transformationists, by contrast, do not speak of gradual change. They believe the world is quickly becoming so different that we will not only act differently, but we will also think differently. What does it mean to think differently?

Try to put your mind back into the time when people believed that Earth was at the center of the universe. Imagine how ideas changed as people realized that Earth is just one small planet circling a medium-sized star toward the edge of the Milky Way galaxy—which itself moves among a hundred billion galaxies in the universe.

Another example of thinking differently: Centuries ago people believed that thinking was done in the heart, rather than in the brain. Living in the twentieth century, I am so accustomed to the idea that I think with my brain that it is very difficult to imagine thinking with my heart. The whole idea seems ridiculous. I sit quietly and try to imagine thinking with my heart. I *really* concentrate. But where do I "feel" myself concentrating? In my head, of course. Mentally, I try to push that "feeling" down from my head into my heart, but it just does not work. I *know* I think with my brain, and I *know* my brain is in my head. So almost before I "feel" thinking in my heart, it pops right back up into my head again. Do you have the same difficulty? It must have been just as difficult to change one's thinking the other way round. In fact, even though the Greek physician Galen conducted experiments to show that the head, not the heart, controlled human activity, a thousand years passed before anyone seriously pursued his idea.

Some futurists say that a transformation at least that difficult and much larger in scope is happening right now. Marilyn Ferguson calls it the "aquarian conspiracy" (referring to the sign of Aquarius in the zodiac). Transformational futurists believe that many people already think in the new way, which focuses on living in harmony with our environment, a sense of unity with all peoples on our globe, and cooperation rather than competition. Soon, they say, everyone will think in this new way. Transformationist and evolutionist, space-oriented and earth-centered, pessimist and optimist—futurists offer many ideas.

CHOOSING AMONG FUTURES

Eventually, futurists may improve their information and methods so that they forecast similar sets of possible futures and understand better how we could make each of those futures happen. Even so, it is not their responsibility to decide which future is better than another. They cannot decide whether it is better to stay on earth or seek to conquer space. They cannot determine whether it is better first to overcome cancer, to make sure that everyone in the world has enough nourishing food, or to end the threat of nuclear war. They may express their opinions on these choices along with the rest of us, but decisions like these are not objective and cannot be settled with scientific methods. Rather, such decisions depend on people's values— what they think is good and what they think is bad.

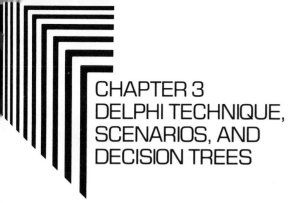

CHAPTER 3
DELPHI TECHNIQUE,
SCENARIOS, AND
DECISION TREES

Chapter 1 described the ways in which fortune-tellers and prophets have tried to look into the future. Their methods, some of which are thousands of years old, are usually based on the assumption that the future is predetermined, that there is only one way the future can happen. Therefore, a fortune-teller tries to see into *the* future—that one and only future.

Modern futurists, however, take a different approach. They know that only one future will really happen for a person when he or she gets there. But looking ahead, futurists can imagine future events leading in several different directions. Therefore, they forecast several alternate futures. Then they suggest which decisions today are most likely to lead to one or another of those possible futures. Chapters 3 and 4 describe some of the methods used to develop and present those alternatives— methods that have been used for about forty years.

DELPHI TECHNIQUE

In chapter 1 you read about the oracle at Delphi in ancient Greece. About twenty-five hundred years ago the priestess at this oracle was consulted even by kings who wanted to know about the future. Do you remember the misfortunes of Croesus?

About thirty years ago futurists named a new method after that ancient oracle. The modern Delphi technique was one of the first attempts to approach futuristics in a scientific way. As you read the following paragraphs, ask yourself how the modern Delphi technique resembles the ancient oracle and how it is different.

The Delphi technique is a method of forecasting possible futures by combining the ideas of several experts on the topic under investigation. To begin a Delphi study, therefore, futurists ask several experts for their opinions on one or more possibilities for the future.

Suppose you wanted to know who is most likely to win your school's next football game—the home team or the visitors. How would you use the opinions of experts to get the best prediction? If you chose to try the Delphi technique to predict the winner, your first step would be to make a list of experts. You might include the coaches of both teams, some team members, a sportscaster or reporter, and maybe one or two students who regularly attend the games. Probably you would not talk directly with the experts; instead, you would ask for a written reply. You would send each expert a written questionnaire with questions like:

- Which team will win the ball game this Saturday between the Hometown Homers and the Valiant Visitors? Or will it be a tie?
- Why do you think so?

The experts will not talk with one another. They will not even know who else is on your list of experts. Instead, they will send their answers straight to you. When all the answers come back, Round One of the Delphi study is complete.

Your next step is to compile the results—to put together a report. To compile the results, you count how many experts predict the game will be a tie, how many expect a home team victory, and how many choose the visitors to win. You also write down the reasons given by various experts.

Next you begin Round Two. You want to find out whether any of the experts will change their forecast when they see how most of the other experts voted and the reasons they gave for their choices. So you send the results of Round One back to your experts. This time you ask:

- Do you want to change your forecast?
- Why or why not?

Suppose that in Round One just one person, your school's coach, predicted that the home team will win. Suppose that the coach's reason is that the best pass receiver on the visitor's team has just been injured in a motorcycle accident. Would that new bit of information lead some of your experts to switch their forecast on Round Two from the visiting team to the home team?

When Round Two results come back, you compile this new information. If opinions change or new reasons turn up, or if you suspect some of your experts may still change their minds, you can go on to Round Three and Round Four.

Forecasting the outcome of a football game is a fairly simple task because, assuming that the game is not called off, there are only three possible outcomes (win, lose, or tie), and only one of those outcomes can happen. Also keeping the task simple is the fact that the players and the rules are well known, and the circumstance that the outcome will be determined at a known time in the future. Delphi studies are often much more complicated than our example of forecasting the winner of a football game.

Suppose you wanted to use the Delphi technique to forecast the championship school football team in the year 2000. How might the Delphi study be different? For one thing, you might ask your experts such questions as:

- Will football be played in the year 2000?
- If so, will the rules be the same or different?
- Will this school still be open at that time? Or rebuilt? Or enlarged?

- Will football players here be any stronger? taller? about the same?
- What food, training techniques, etc., will be available?

The forecasts called for in looking ahead to the year 2000 are much more difficult and more complicated than in who will win or lose the next game. It might take several Delphi rounds to put together a forecast about the year 2000. Several different forecasts may be developed—one in case the school stays open and another in which the school would be closed; one in case genetic engineering or diet changes physical abilities and another if not; perhaps even one in case some of the team members come from another planet.

The Delphi method has been used to forecast possibilities in space travel, politics, inventions, the environment, education, and many other areas. This technique brings together the opinions and knowledge of a number of people who ought to know what they are talking about. The next time you want to explore something about the future, you may want to try a Delphi study.

SCENARIOS

We have found that the Delphi technique is a means of combining the ideas of experts to forecast the future, or several future possibilities. A SCENARIO is not so much a way of forecasting future possibilities as a way of telling about them. Just as a movie scenario describes the setting and tells what happens in a particular movie, so a futuristic scenario describes a future world and tells what might have happened to create that world. Notice that the word SCENARIO is much like the word SCENE—in fact, a scenario describes a future scene.

Often just one expert works alone to write a scenario, or several scenarios. Sometimes, however, a group of experts may develop a scenario. Unlike the experts in a Delphi study, the authors of a scenario usually work together.

Imagine a party, a test, a sports event, or some other happening in which you will be involved within the next week or so. If you were to write down a description of what you think that happening will be like and what will occur, your description would be a scenario. If you are beginning to think like a futurist, you would write not just one, but two or three scenarios, because you would think of more than one way the happening might turn out.

To get ideas for a scenario, futurists may use the results of a Delphi study, a decision tree, trend extrapolations, or other techniques. (You will read about decision trees and trend extrapolation later.) By putting such information into a page or two of description, futurists make the future world seem more real to us. They fill in details and show how certain decisions today are likely to lead, step by step, to a particular future situation. They often write several different scenarios to help us choose the situation that looks best and then make decisions so the best scenario is likely to come true.

Authors of science fiction stories set in the future imagine the worlds of their stories, too (as mentioned in chapter 1). Take, for example, the book NOONAN by Leonard Everett Fisher. In this humorous story Johnny Noonan is bumped on the head in a baseball game and regains consciousness a hundred years later. He is then an outstanding pitcher because he can control the baseball with ESP. A scenario for NOONAN reads like this:

> The year is 1996. Back in 1983 the world changed when all the oil wells ran dry. The Russians cried foul until the same thing happened to their own wells in the Ukraine. The United Nations was unable to solve the problem. From 1983 to 1989 scientists everywhere worked frantically to develop new sources of energy, while Americans spent all their spare time at home watching television. By 1990, however, a solution was found.
>
> Meanwhile, baseball has changed, never again to return to its former state. During the 1980's the great stadiums were stripped of their seats, walled in, and

roofed over. Now, everyone watches baseball at home on pay TV, and the ball parks are giant-sized TV studios. Games begin, not when an umpire yells "Play Ball," but when the television director points at the pitcher. There is only one real ball park left—Wrigley Field in Chicago. Secretly, every ballplayer wants to play in Wrigley Field. The roar of the crowds is marvelous, almost symphonic— not to mention the fresh air.*

This scenario not only describes a future world, but also tells how it came to be that way.

The next example, also from science fiction, reads like history written at a future time. TREASURES OF MORROW by H. M. Hoover tells a story of earth in the twenty-fifth century. The following scenario, paraphrased from the novel, tells how our world changed, as imagined by the novelist.

It began when pollution reached a level earth's atmosphere could no longer absorb. The seas turned gray, then brown and thick with scum. Ugly clouds of smog layered in heavy stillness over the cities, endlessly drizzling dirty rain. As the oceans' enormous masses of plankton slowly died from the filth man continuously spewed into the water, as the oxygen supply generated by the plankton diminished, as the plants and trees on the land sickened and turned brown or yellow, the chain of life began to break, link by link. In the decade known as The Death of the Seas, over 93 percent of all living creatures on the earth's surface and under the seas died by simple suffocation. In the twenty-fourth century enormous earthquakes lowered parts of California up to 12 feet (3.6 m), raised the Chilean Andes a corresponding distance, and devastated Japan.

Hidden in a secret underground complex called LIFE-SPAN, a small group survived. They had retained the

*Leonard Everett Fisher, NOONAN (New York: Avon, 1981).

knowledge and adapted the technology of the old world. But they had also become a highly intelligent race of telepaths. Six generations after The Death of the Seas the people emerged from LIFESPAN into an oxygen-thin atmosphere and began living on the surface of the earth near what had once been San Diego, California. They thought themselves alone on earth, but they were mistaken.*

Does this scenario give a clear picture of this future world? Can you see it in your imagination? If so, how did the writer make the scenario seem real?

Of course, a writer of a science fiction scenario, unlike a futurist, may not worry about whether the scenario could really happen. An author of science fiction is an imagineer, as discussed in chapter 1, rather than a futurist. Both science fiction writers and futurists, however, play with ideas about the future.

The science fiction scenario you just read is in the past tense; words like BEGAN, TURNED and DIED tell the reader to think these events have already happened. A past tense scenario is sometimes called "future history" because it is written as though someone from the future were telling the history of events up to that time.

However, whether developed by an imagineer or by a futurist, scenarios may also be written in the present or in the future tense. Let us compare the three tenses. A scenario in the past tense begins this way:

By 1994 helicopters had replaced automobiles. About that time Lee Santos established the Santos Helicab Company. . . .

Since most stories, news items, and history books are written in the past tense, the reader is prepared to believe, or at least to pretend to believe, such a scenario.

*H. M. Hoover, TREASURES OF MORROW (New York: Four Winds Press, 1976).

The same idea in the present tense begins:

It is 1994. Helicopters are more widely used than the automobile. Lee Santos is president of the Santos Helicab Company. . . .

Notice that the present tense makes readers feel that the situation is occurring right before their eyes.

In the future tense the passage reads:

In 1994 helicopters will replace automobiles. Lee Santos will become president of the Santos Helicab Company. . . .

Since we are talking about the future, the future tense seems natural. A writer must choose the tense best fitted to his or her ideas and to the readers of the scenario. To feel the effect of each tense, you might want to use each version as a "story starter" and create your own adventures for Lee Santos.

Scenarios are especially useful to describe and compare two or three possible futures. Scenarios have been used to describe world, national, or business futures for those who make decisions in government and industry. These people often do not have time to study pages and pages of statistics and charts. A scenario gives them a short, understandable description of the world they may create by the decisions they make.

Scenarios are also helpful in putting ourselves into a futurist frame of mind. We can imagine ourselves walking right into a scenario more easily than we can see ourselves in a trend extrapolation or a computer simulation. Thinking of ourselves in a future world may be even easier if the scenario is presented in a drawing or motion picture.

Scenarios help us realize how much the world may change in the next twenty or thirty years. For example, bus drivers may no longer be needed if buses work automatically, or if they are replaced by "moving sidewalks." At the same time, though, more pilots may be needed to fly shuttles to and from space stations that become vacation spots circling the earth in outer space.

What other jobs may disappear or be created in the future? A scenario can describe such changes.

Can you imagine a setting for a science fiction story set in future time? And then think about what would happen to bring that situation about? Perhaps you would enjoy writing a couple of paragraphs about that world to create your own science fiction scenario.

DECISION TREES

Futurists know that the future may turn out in one of several different ways. Choices made today affect future possibilities. One way to work through a set of choices is to chart them in a decision tree. Each branch in such a chart represents a choice one might make and leads to a future outcome, or several possible outcomes. A decision tree looks very much like a flow chart you may have seen or designed for a computer program.

Suppose that you plan to go out Saturday night. You have just received your driver's license, so one possibility is to borrow Mom's car. How could you chart the possible strategies—and alternate plans—to help you decide how you want to proceed? Here is a decision tree that shows two strategies for borrowing Mom's car so you can go out next Saturday. One possibility is to ask right away; the other is to wait until Saturday afternoon.

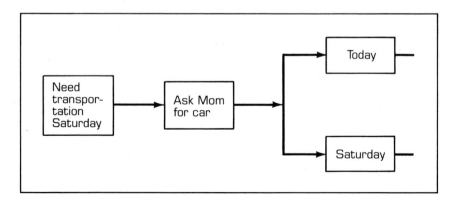

If you ask today, Mom may say yes, no, or maybe. If you wait until Saturday to ask she will not have much time to think it over, so probably she will say yes or no right away. Of course, if today she says maybe, you can ask her again later in the week. With these possibilities the decision tree looks like the one on page 43:

Notice the little bump in the connection from "maybe" to the Saturday line. The bump means the two lines do not touch one another.

In any case, if the answer is yes, you will be able to use Mom's car, but what happens if she says no? Look at the diagram on page 44.

Whether you ask now or wait, the decision tree shows that if Mom says no, you are left with a question mark, meaning no transportation. So it might be wise to have some other possibilities in mind. What two additional transportation possibilities are suggested in the following decision tree?

Working out a decision tree is somewhat like working out a puzzle. Can you copy this diagram on another sheet of paper and show all the choices that arise in taking Mom's car? In riding with a friend? In taking the bus? Look at the diagram on page 45.

For one way to finish the diagram, turn to page 46.

As the diagram on page 46 indicates, even a fairly simple problem turns into quite a complicated decision tree. The decision tree itself does not show which decision is the best, but it provides a technique for following through all the possible choices and then examining them in a visual display.

As you study this tree, other possibilities may come to mind. For example, one might arrange with a friend for a ride even if Mom says maybe when she is asked right away. If she says yes later on, one could cancel the arrangements with the friend.

In studying this decision tree, you would also want to consider which is the PREFERRED result. Would you rather borrow Mom's car, ride with a friend, or take a bus? Suppose you prefer to borrow Mom's car. Then you could trace in red the paths that lead to borrowing Mom's car and focus your attention on those steps.

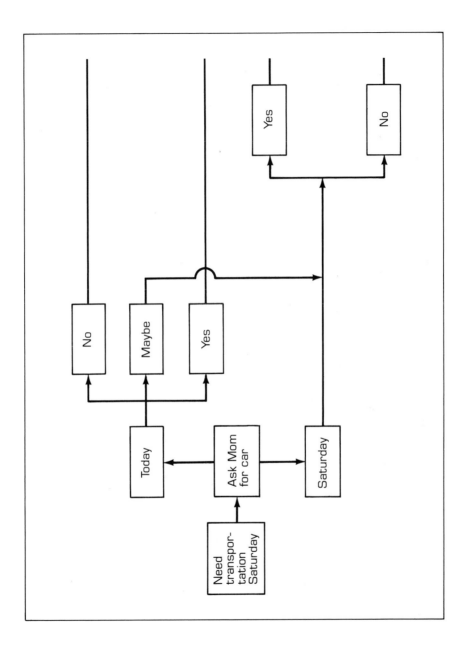

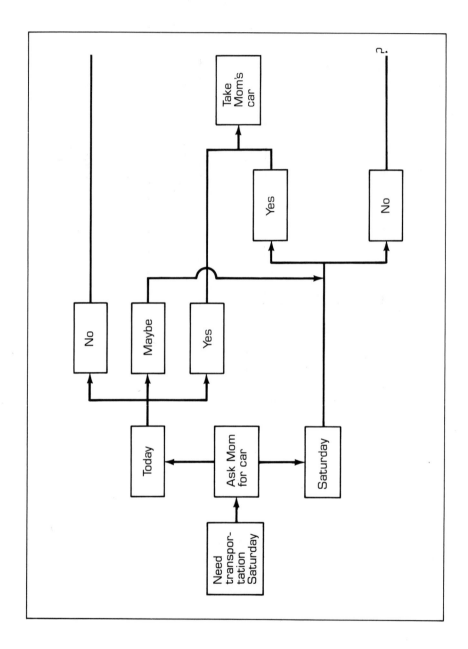

[44]

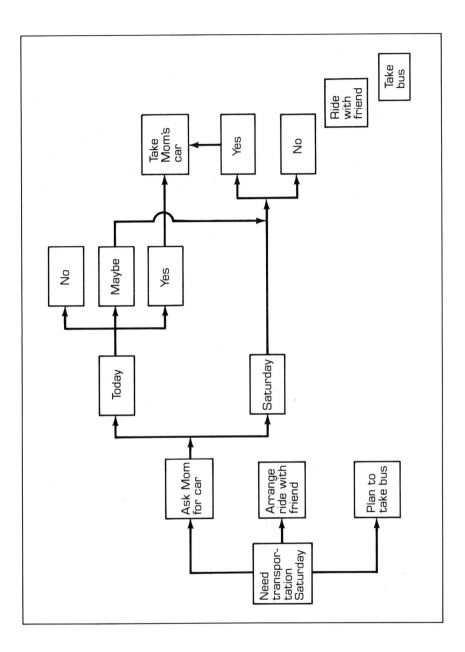

[45]

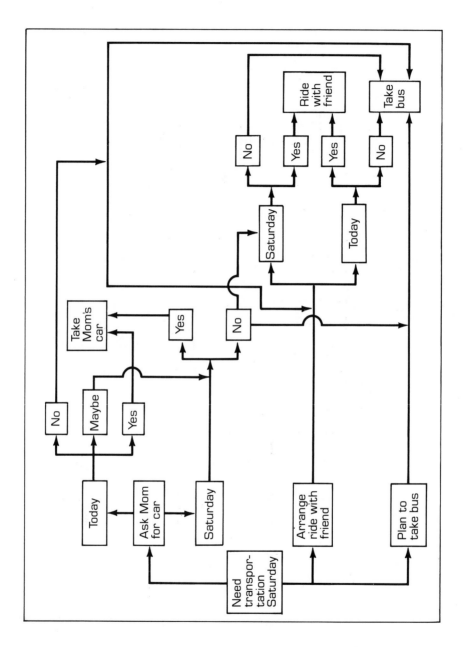

In addition, you might think about which choices are *most likely* to lead to the preferred outcome. Perhaps if you ask Mom now, she is most likely to say maybe, worry for a few days, and finally say no. On the other hand, if you wait until the day you want the car to ask for it, Mom may have made plans of her own.

Other important information may be missing from the diagram. For example, if you take the bus, you will spend only fifty cents. If you ride with your friend, you may need only to chip in for gas. But if you take Mom's car, you might pay for all the gas and be expected to wash and polish the car on Sunday besides. All these factors may affect your final decision.

A decision tree is a useful device for charting various courses of action. It can be used for planning, as well as for decision making, in which case it is sometimes called a relevance tree. For example, NASA used a relevance tree to plan how scientists would analyze materials retrieved from the moon by the Apollo spacecraft.

If the diagram becomes too complicated, a computer may be used to follow up on all the choices and even to calculate which is most likely to yield the desired result. Decision trees are useful because they show various actions and their effects on one another in a single diagram.

Perhaps right now you are facing a decision, or trying to figure out how to get a particular thing accomplished, or how to solve a problem. Why not try a decision tree? Your best course of action may become clear to you as you diagram the steps and possibilities.

CHAPTER 4
TREND
EXTRAPOLATION

TREND EXTRAPOLATION is a method of futuristics that is often quoted in newspapers and broadcasts. For example, a news article may indicate that if the world continues to use oil at the same rate as in the last five years, all oil reserves would be used up in a certain length of time. Such a statement is the result of trend extrapolation.

Like the Delphi technique, trend extrapolation is a way of using information presently available to make predictions about the future. However, instead of using the opinions of experts, trend extrapolation usually depends upon statistical information, that is, on numbers. When using trend extrapolation, futurists first look for a pattern—called a "trend." Then they extend—or extrapolate—that trend into the future. In other words, trend extrapolation is a way of looking toward the future by carrying forward an existing pattern.

Suppose that last weekend you had a two-hour baby-sitting job and made ten dollars. The family you worked for told some friends, so this weekend you have two jobs like that. Let us try trend extrapolation to forecast your future jobs and income as a baby-sitter.

So far you have had two hours of baby-sitting and a ten-dollar income the first weekend—followed by four hours of baby-sitting and a twenty-dollar income the second weekend.

Weekend	Baby-Sitting	Income
#1	2 hours	$10
#2	4 hours	$20

Look for a pattern. Perhaps the trend is to add two hours of baby-sitting each weekend. If so, how many hours would you baby-sit on weekend #3? How much money would you make? How about weekend #4?

If you think you can expect to add two hours of baby-sitting each week, your trend extrapolation will look like this:

Chart
A

Weekend	Baby-Sitting	Income
#1	2 hours	$10
#2	4 hours	$20
#3	6 hours	$30
#4	8 hours	$40
#5	10 hours	$50
#6	12 hours	$60
#7	14 hours	$70

(and so on)

By the seventh weekend you are baby-sitting fourteen hours and earning seventy dollars. Or, putting the same extrapolation into the form of a graph:

[50]

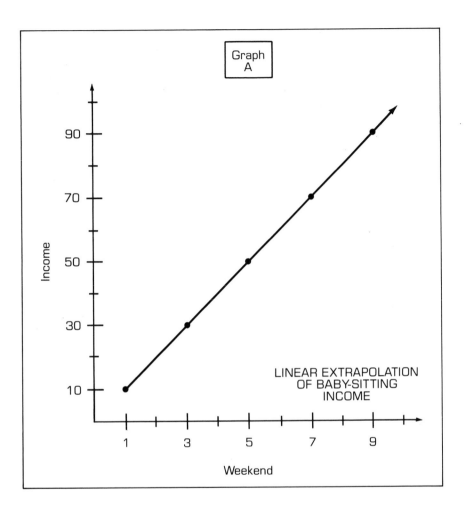

Notice that adding the same amount each week produces a graph which is a straight line. For this reason, a trend which ADDS the same number each time is called a linear trend, and the extrapolation is a linear extrapolation. It looks as if the line could continue climbing upwards indefinitely. But as we shall see in a few more paragraphs, that is not possible.

Look back at the first two weekends (page 50) for another pattern. Perhaps the trend is to DOUBLE the baby-sitting each week, rather than just to add two hours. In that case, how many hours would you baby-sit on weekend #3? How much money would you make? How about weekend #4?

To extrapolate a trend of DOUBLING the baby-sitting hours and income each weekend, you multiply by two each week. The chart looks like this:

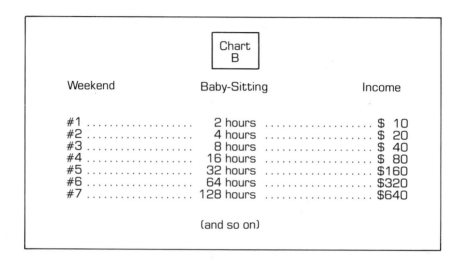

Chart B

Weekend	Baby-Sitting	Income
#1	2 hours	$ 10
#2	4 hours	$ 20
#3	8 hours	$ 40
#4	16 hours	$ 80
#5	32 hours	$160
#6	64 hours	$320
#7	128 hours	$640

(and so on)

By the seventh weekend you are baby-sitting 128 hours and earning $640. (Careful! How many hours are in a weekend? We will check this out in a moment.)

Opposite is the doubling extrapolation in graph form:

By the sixth weekend you are baby-sitting sixty-four hours and earning $320. The seventh weekend goes right off the top of our graph, the line is climbing so fast! Such a trend, produced by MULTIPLICATION, is called a geometric trend. (The reason the term "geometric" is used relates to the way area increases in a geometric shape. For example, if the side of a square is mul-

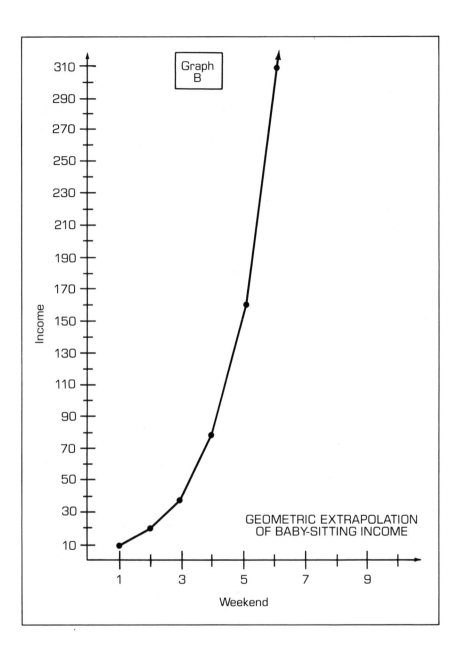

Graph
B

GEOMETRIC EXTRAPOLATION
OF BABY-SITTING INCOME

Income

Weekend

tiplied by two, its area becomes four times larger. If the side of the same square is multiplied by four, the area becomes sixteen times larger, and so on.)

There are two important points to notice about the baby-sitting futures shown in Charts A and B. The first point is that Chart B is already impossible by weekend #6. There are only about sixty hours in a weekend (Friday evening, Saturday, and Sunday), but on weekend #6 in Chart B you are being paid for sixty-four hours. Even if you were sleeping overnight in the house where you were working, you probably would not be paid the full five dollars an hour overnight. And on weekend #7 you would be baby-sitting one hundred twenty-eight hours— impossible!

So there are sometimes limits to extrapolations. Even on Chart A you would eventually reach a limit. By weekend #30 on Chart A you would be baby-sitting all sixty hours of the weekend and could not continue to add more hours. Thus, a linear extrapolation may go on for a longer period of time than a geometric extrapolation from the same starting point, but after a while the linear trend, too, is likely to reach a limit.

Sports provide other examples of limits. Let us consider the "four-minute mile." Once it was thought that no one could run a mile in less than four minutes. Official records begin with a time of nearly five minutes in 1864. Greater skill in training, better nutrition, and other factors have gradually shortened that time. Look at the set of records at the top of page 55 (Chart C). In the first ten years, from 1864 to 1874, the mile was run just thirty seconds faster—half a minute. Suppose someone back in 1874 had made a linear extrapolation like Chart A and Graph A for the baby-sitting problem. That extrapolation would have forecast a four-minute mile in about 1883, and a one-mile run in zero minutes—no time at all—before 1965 (see Graph C). Clearly, it is impossible to run a mile in no time at all. The linear extrapolation goes beyond the limits of the possible.

But look back to Chart C to find out what really happened. Even though thirty seconds were taken off the record in just TEN years, another EIGHTY years passed before Roger Bannister took off twenty-six seconds more to "break" the four-minute

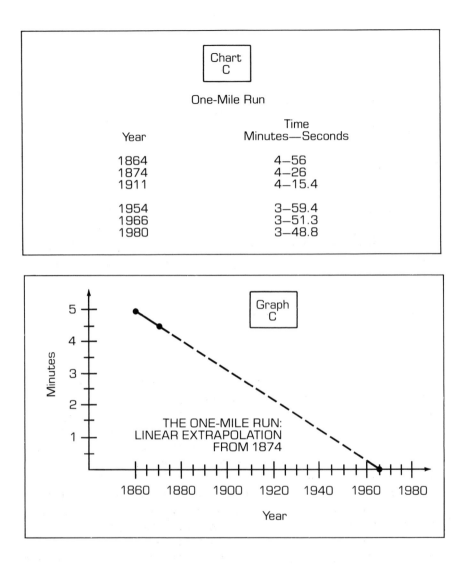

Chart
C

One-Mile Run

Year	Time Minutes—Seconds
1864	4–56
1874	4–26
1911	4–15.4
1954	3–59.4
1966	3–51.3
1980	3–48.8

Graph
C

THE ONE-MILE RUN:
LINEAR EXTRAPOLATION
FROM 1874

mile. In the twenty-six years from 1954 to 1980 only eleven more seconds were shaved off the record. The real history of the one-mile run is reflected in Graph D on page 56.

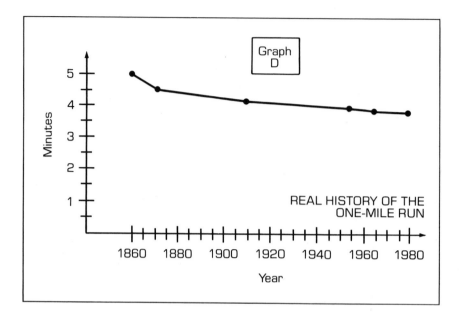

Graph
D

5

4

3

2

1

Minutes

REAL HISTORY OF THE
ONE-MILE RUN

1860   1880   1900   1920   1940   1960   1980

Year

The line on Graph D becomes flatter and flatter because it took longer and longer to beat the record by, say, a quarter of a minute. The mile can never be run in no time at all. Will it ever be run in one minute? Two minutes? The trend is coming to its limit, at which time it will graph as a straight, horizontal line. Limits are important to keep in mind when doing extrapolations.

There is a second important point to notice about the baby-sitting future produced in Charts A and B, and that is the fact that two different futures are shown there (alternate futures) because two different patterns, or trends, could be seen in the first two weekends. But if we had waited until the fourth or fifth weekend, one of those patterns would no longer have fit the facts. On the other hand, a different trend, or trends, might have been suggested.

The next time you are involved in a project that is gradually changing, you may want to try trend extrapolation to see what you can expect as the project develops. Your project might be learning to type faster, gaining or losing weight, writing a term paper, or persuading other studends to vote for a particular candidate in your class election. Is there something you can count or measure about the project as it goes along? Do you see any pattern in the numbers you get as you count or measure? What will happen if that pattern continues? Is there anything that will make a limit beyond which the pattern cannot continue? And afterward—did your project come along as the extrapolation forecast? Could you have found a different pattern to make a better forecast? Did the extrapolation help you in carrying out the project?

Futurists use trend extrapolations to look for patterns—not only linear and geometric, but also cycles and other more complicated trends. (An example of a cycle might be a drought every three years which reduces production of wheat.) A trend may be expressed as a mathematical equation. With such trends in mind, futurists develop extrapolations on such topics as population, food production, oil resources, and income. They may forecast how much energy we will be using in the year 2000, how much energy will be produced, and then whether or not the world will be in short supply for its energy needs.

Different trends may seem possible, leading to alternate futures, as was true in the baby-sitting data. Or futurists may disagree on how much one trend will be influenced by another. Most important, very little is known about limits of various sorts and how they will change extrapolations. Often futurists do not have enough long-term information to help them identify trends or develop extrapolations. Sometimes the factors that could affect a trend are very numerous and complicated.

Also, world conditions are always changing, so trends may change. Individuals and governments sometimes make decisions that are intended to change trends. For instance, when automobile manufacturers in the United States began to lose money in the late 1970s, those companies offered discounts, slowed production, and took other steps intended to reverse that trend and help them make a profit. A futurist who did not expect those changes would have made incorrect forecasts, just as weather forecasters would describe the weather incorrectly if they did not know about a storm heading their way. Therefore, trend extrapolation must be used with caution. With all these complications and changes, it is not surprising that trend extrapolations often lead futurists to forecast not just one future, but several alternate futures.

POSTSCRIPT: THINKING LIKE A FUTURIST

The phrase "future shock" was invented by Alvin Toffler. In medicine a person "goes into shock" after an accident or some other serious event. A physical change comes so quickly that the body has trouble adjusting. A person in shock may become very ill. Toffler's "future shock" is not an illness or emergency, like a medical case of shock, but it IS a response to change. People in "future shock" feel confused and helpless because they are overwhelmed by too many changes in too short a time. One way to avoid future shock is to think like a futurist. And just how is that?

Some students that Toffler knew did NOT think like futurists. He asked them to list changes they could foresee in the future, and they listed many changes, from control of disease to travel to other planets. But when Toffler asked them to list the jobs they would hold as adults, they listed all the same old jobs that have been available for years. They did not see that changes in technology would make some jobs obsolete and create different occupations. Well then, how does a futurist think?

First of all—obviously—futurists think about the future. They think ahead about their lives and about the world.

Second, futurists gather and study as much useful information as they can whenever they must decide something important.

Third, futurists think about what will happen as a consequence of decisions we make today—not only consequences for next week or next year, but also for ten or a hundred years from now. They know things are interconnected, so that a change here causes other changes there and there and over there.

Fourth, futurists know that alternate futures lie before us, not just one. They think about what future will be best.

Fifth, futurists understand that we choose the kind of future we want according to our values or beliefs about what is good or bad. Therefore, it is important to think carefully about what we believe.

Finally, futurists know that decisions made today influence how the future will really happen. So they do what they can to work toward a better future for the world. They agree with Max Lerner, a writer for TIME magazine, who said that we should not be pessimists, always looking on the bad side of things. Neither should we be optimists, always looking on the good side. Instead, we should be possibilists, believing that everything depends on using our wisdom to make choices and then our determination to follow through.

GLOSSARY

CHIROMANCY (ký ra mań see): palm reading.

DELPHI (del' fy): ancient town on the side of Mount Parnassus in Greece, home of the Delphic oracle.

DIVINATION (dĭv' ĭ nay' shun): the practice of foretelling the future by interpreting omens or signs.

DIVINER (dĭ vyn' er): a person who can prophesy the future.

DYSTOPIA (diss toe' pee ah): a story in which the human condition is at its lowest; the opposite of utopia.

EVOLUTIONIST (ev a lu' shan ist): one who believes that the future will develop gradually from the present, as the present has from the past.

FUTURISTS (few' tyer ists): people who study information about the past and present in order to forecast some of the many futures that could possibly happen.

IMAGINEERS (ĭ maj' ĭ neers'): people who use their imaginations to write descriptions and stories of the future.

ORACLE (or' ah kul): the place where a god or goddess was thought to reveal the future; the person who announced such predictions.

PASTORAL UTOPIA (you toé pee ah): a story of a return to a simpler way of life.

PHILOSOPHERS (fĭ lahs' ah fers): people who think about why things are and how they should be.

PHRENOLOGY (fri nol' o jee): studying the shape of the head to determine character and mental abilities.

PRECOGNITION (pre' cog nĭ' shun): the ability to see or hear future events before they occur; a form of extrasensory perception, or ESP.

PROPHET (prof' ĭt): a religious person who foretells future events.

PSYCHIC (sy' kick): a person who has the ability to see or hear future events before they occur.

SCENARIO (see nar' ee oh): an account of a possible future course of action or world.

TAROT (tar' oh) CARDS: fortune-telling cards.

THINK TANK: An organization, department, or group of experts who study the future.

TRANSFORMATIONIST (trans for ma' shan ist): a person who believes that the world is changing so fast that we will not only act differently in the future, but we will also think differently.

TREND EXTRAPOLATION (ex trap' o' lay' shun): using information presently available to make predictions about the future.

UTOPIA (you toe' pee ah): a perfect country.

FOR FUTURE READING

Abels, Harriette S. OUR FUTURE WORLD SERIES. Mankato, Minn.: Crestwood House, 1980.

Ardley, Neil. AT SCHOOL, WORK AND PLAY. The World of Tomorrow Series. New York: Franklin Watts, 1982.

———. TOMORROW'S HOME. The World of Tomorrow Series. New York: Franklin Watts, 1982.

Baldwin, Margaret and Gary Pack. ROBOTS AND ROBOTICS. New York: Franklin Watts, 1984.

Cornish, Edward. THE STUDY OF THE FUTURE. Washington, D.C.: World Future Society, 1977.

Douglas, John H. and the Editors of Grolier. THE FUTURE WORLD OF ENERGY. Walt Disney World EPCOT Center Series. New York: Franklin Watts, 1984.

Edelson, Edward. THE BOOK OF PROPHECY. Garden City, N.Y.: Doubleday, 1974.

THE FUTURIST. Magazine published by the World Future Society.

Gay, Kathlyn. ACID RAIN. New York: Franklin Watts, 1983.

Gurney, Gene. SPACE TECHNOLOGY SPINOFFS. NEW YORK: FRANKLIN WATTS, 1979.

Horwitz, Elinor Lander. THE SOOTHSAYER'S HANDBOOK—A GUIDE TO BAD SIGNS & GOOD VIBRATIONS. Philadelphia: Lippincott, 1972.

Hoyle, Geoffrey. 2010: LIVING IN THE FUTURE. Illus. by Alastair Anderson. New York: Parents Magazine Press, 1973.

Lampton, Christopher. FUSION: THE ETERNAL FLAME. New York: Franklin Watts, 1982.

Lely, James A. STAR TREK. Mankato, Minn.: Creative Education, 1979.

————.STAR WARS. Mankato, Minn.: Creative Education, 1979.

Murphy, Wendy and the Editors of Grolier. THE FUTURE WORLD OF AGRICULTURE. Walt Disney World EPCOT Center Series. New York: Franklin Watts, 1984.

Sagan, Carl. COSMOS. New York: Random House, 1980.

Taylor, L. B., Jr. SPACE: BATTLEGROUND OF THE FUTURE? New York: Franklin Watts, 1983.

Taylor, Paula. THE KIDS' WHOLE FUTURE CATALOG. New York: Random House, 1982.

INDEX